The People of Twelve Thousand Winters

Written by **Trinka Hakes Noble** and Illustrated by **Jim Madsen**

Tales of the World *from* Sleeping Bear Press

AMERICA

For Joy, David, Lizzie, and Dylan, with love.

T.H.N.

◈

For Holly, Mckenzie, Hannah, and Easton—my family.

Jim

Sleeping Bear Press
315 E. Eisenhower Parkway, Suite 200
Ann Arbor, MI 48108
www.sleepingbearpress.com

Sleeping Bear Press is an imprint of Gale, a part of Cengage Learning.

10 9 8 7 6 5 4 3 2 1

Printed by China Translation & Printing Services Limited,
Guangdong Province, China. 1st printing.   11/2011

Library of Congress Cataloging-in-Publication Data

Noble, Trinka Hakes.
The people of twelve thousand winters / Trinka Hakes Noble ;
illustrated by Jim Masdsen.
p. cm.
ISBN 978-1-58536-529-6
1.Delaware Indians—Juvenile literature.I. Madsen, Jim, 1964- ill.
II. Title.
E99.D2N64 2011
974.004`97345—dc23
                              2011030796

We are the Lenni Lenape, which means "we the people." Through the snows of twelve thousand winters we have kept our fires burning. To me, twelve thousand winters is a long, long time. I, myself, am only ten winters. I am Walking Turtle.

At my naming ceremony the *wayhuhweehuhlahs,* the giver of names, told my mother, Half Moon Dancer, "He shall carry his people on his back, as steady and sure as a hard-shelled turtle that walks over land toward water. He shall be Walking Turtle Boy."

Walking Turtle is a good name for me because I carry my cousin, Little Talk, on my back wherever we go. Little Talk was born with a crooked foot. His legs did not grow straight and strong like mine. He speaks little, but talks to me. "*Wanisi*, thank you, Walking Turtle," he says.

I am the one who should say *wanisi*. Carrying Little Talk has made me strong.

Last summer, in the time of the Green Corn, I had grown strong enough to carry Little Talk all the way down the Minisink Trail to the Great Salt Sea where Brother Sun rises to greet our people each morning. Otherwise, he would have stayed behind to scare the crows from the corn.

But my feet are happiest walking the ancient forest pathways that have carried the footprints of my people for centuries. Giant oaks, sturdy chestnuts, and towering elms stand guard above me. Cawing crows announce my presence. On the forest floor, woodland ferns gently swish their shy greeting against my legs.

From the hill above our village, I can see blue wood smoke drift up into the late summer dusk. Below, our Passaic River glistens in the silvery gray light. Grandmother waves from the door of our lodge. She keeps our fires burning.

We are a three-fire lodge. Grandmother's fire is at the end of the lodge, my family's fire is in the middle, and Little Talk's family fire is by the door. Three smoke holes are at the top and our door faces east to greet the rising sun. We sleep on platforms around the edge. Little Talk and I sleep on one side with the tops of our heads together. Heart Berry, my little sister, sleeps at my feet. Father and Mother sleep on the other side of our fire.

Mother wakes early. She hurries into the forest to gather wild onions, sage, and berries in her big cooking pot. Heart Berry follows, filling her little pot with wild grapes, vine berries, and the last few wild strawberries, her namesake. And just like Heart Berry, they are sweet with no thorns.

I carry wood so Grandmother can prepare our outdoor cooking fire. Tonight we will have a hot stew of dried venison, cornmeal, wild onions, and Heart Berry's sweet fruits of the forest.

In the Time of the Falling Leaves everyone is busy. This is our gathering time. Squash and pumpkin rings dry in the autumn sun. Rows of braided corn already hang in our lodge. Bark baskets of dried beans are stored under our sleeping platforms. It is as though our Mother the Earth has moved into our lodge.

In the afternoon, all the women and children go into the forest to gather hickory nuts, black walnuts, chestnuts, and acorns. It is hard work, but the women sing and the children are given time to play. Heart Berry strings acorns to make little dolls. Little Talk and I play *kokolesh,* Cup and Pin, a game he is good at.

But when I return to our village carrying Little Talk and our baskets, Father frowns. Later, he takes me to a lone lodge at the edge of our village down by the river.

"Walking Turtle," Father says sternly, "in just one more winter you will come here to warrior school."

I shiver as the trainer makes the boys plunge into the icy water to swim beyond the river's bend and back. Next they hold their breath and run as far as they can to make them long-winded. My lungs burn as I try to hold my breath as long as they do. Near the fire, some boys are trying to catch corn pone on the end of a pointed stick. If they miss, they do not eat. I see the hunger in their eyes.

Then Father speaks. "Walking Turtle, here in warrior school you will face many tests. You will learn the ways of a great hunter, a proud and brave warrior. It will not be easy." Father crosses his arms in silence, a sign his words are finished.

But I know what his unspoken words are saying. I must come to warrior school but Little Talk cannot. How can I come here without Little Talk?

Inside, I do not like this, but I answer with respect, "*Ahikta nux.* Yes, my Father. I know."

Father is Soaring Hawk. He is well respected in our village as a fair and honest trader. He has traveled as far west as *Shamokin* on the great Susquehanna River and as far south as *Shackamaxon*, the center of *Lenapehoking*. He trades our fine beaver pelts, deerskins, antler pipes, and seashell beads that Grandmother makes. Sometimes he brings back things from afar like a woodland buffalo robe.

Someday, if I do well in warrior school, I will go with him. But I worry about Little Talk when I am gone.

Tonight is our Giving Thanks Ceremony in the Big House. Everyone sits with their own clan. Little Talk, Heart Berry, and I sit behind our mothers and grandmother. We are of the Turtle Clan. Father sits with the Wolf Clan and Little Talk's father sits with the Turkey Clan. But we are all Lenape. We the people have gathered to give thanks to *Kishelemukong*, our Creator.

It is a chilly night. Mother makes us wear our leggings. She wears her turkey feather cape. Her long black hair is dressed with a shell comb and she has painted small red dots on her cheeks and eyelids. I think she looks beautiful.

Like most of the hunters and warriors, Father's face is painted part black and part red in honor of *Mesingw*, the Good Spirit Being of the forest who keeps watch over all the trees, plants, and animals. A special dancer wearing a bearskin and the mask of *Mesingw* appears to remind the people to be grateful to *Mesingw*, especially for the hunters' safe return.

Then, the Big House grows silent, waiting for White Antler. White Antler is our *sakima*.

All at once, our drums begin to beat. Louder and louder they pound until they become the very heartbeat of the earth. My heart beats with the drums until it is pounding, too. Suddenly the drums go silent, and my heart seems to stop.

There stands White Antler, dressed in the head, antlers, and hide of a huge white stag, with dried deer hooves tied above each knee. They jangle as he dances from one end of the Big House to the other, shaking a turtle shell rattle in his hand. Little Talk and I watch every move until White Antler stops in front of our carved center pole.

"Lenape, first people of the sunrise. Listen well to my words."

"*Kishelemukong*, our Creator, has given our people a land that stretches far beyond our Great Salt Sea and Sky Blue Mountains. I have seen the valley of our Ohio brothers and the Big Waters of Michigane. I have heard of the long river of the Mississippi people that divides and washes wide places of grass. I have heard of high mountain peaks of purple that stand guard over other valleys crowded with giant trees and rivers that flow down to another Great Salt Sea where Brother Sun sleeps each night.

"We the people, first to welcome Brother Sun, must be ever grateful to *Kishelemukong* for this vast land beyond our mountains. We must show our thanks by being the caretakers of this bountiful land, in harmony with *Kishelemukong*."

Our drums start to beat. Our people begin to dance. Then Little Talk whispers, "Walking Turtle, carry me up to the thinking place."

Unnoticed, we slip out of the Big House into the night air. We climb the hill above our village and perch on a big overhanging rock. A cold wind blows from the north as gray clouds race across the starry sky. My mind races too, thinking about warrior school and Little Talk and White Antler's words.

Could there be two boys like us on top of those purple mountains, gazing up at the same stars? Could two boys be finding shells in the white salty sand where Brother Sun sleeps? Could White Antler be right? Are we the caretakers? Is this why I must go to warrior school?

I stare up at the Great White Path, searching the ancient stars for an answer. But the stars are silent as they arch across the night sky.

Little Talk must have been thinking much too because he began to speak in a voice that almost sounded like White Antler.

"Walking Turtle," he says, "you have given me your strong back, your straight legs, your kind heart. You have given me the life of a boy I may never have known. Little Talk is grateful to Walking Turtle. In return, I give you my thoughts."

Little Talk pauses, then speaks softly. "Walking Turtle, you are strong. You must go to warrior school. So, I am giving you back your straight legs, your strong back, and your kind heart to take with you. Our people need you to be a brave warrior, a strong leader, and kind caretaker in harmony with *Kishelemukong*. As you have carried me, someday I think you will carry our people into that vast land beyond our Sky Blue Mountains."

A silent time passes between us. Then Little Talk yawns and so do I. It is very late and we are sleepy. As I start down the path, the thickening gray clouds close in and a light snow begins to fall. In no time, Little Talk is sound asleep on my back. But, at that moment, I think Little Talk is the stronger one. It feels like Little Talk is carrying me.

Below, the first snowfall of winter lightly covers our bark lodges. My people are still gathered around fires, telling the stories of old, the drums beating softly now. Someday I too will tell the tale of this night, but for now I am thankful for one more snowfall to add to the snows of twelve thousand winters. One more winter has come to the Lenni Lenape.

We the people will keep our fires burning.

Author's Note

I live on a hill above the Passaic River in northern New Jersey. As I hike the woodland trails behind my studio, I've always felt a respectful and close kinship to the original people who lived here so long ago, the Munsee Lenape. At a bend in the river is a place called Flat Rock where the water flows into many shallow rock pools. It is believed that the Lenape women washed their clothes and utensils here while their children played; it is the same place where we bring our neighborhood children to explore and play in the shallow water.

The timelessness of these ancient New Jersey hills, the endless flow of the river, the gentle wind rising up from the valley floor to shake the dried beech leaves like a Lenape turtle shell rattle has inspired me to dream of a boy named Walking Turtle and his life as an original American. So I set this story here, in this ancient land of the Lenape, where Brother Sun rises up from the Great Salt Sea each morning to greet this land we call America, this place where I live . . . this place where the spirit of the first Americans endures.

—Trinka Hakes Noble

Glossary

The Great White Path: The Milky Way

Heart Berry: The Lenape called wild strawberries "heart berries" because they were red and shaped like a heart.

Kishelemukong (Kish-e-le-mu-kong): Lenape name for God, or the Great Creator

Kokolesh (Ko-ko-lesh): Cup and Pin, a game of skill

Lenni Lenape (Len-ni Le-na-pe): The original people who inhabited New Jersey, southeastern New York, western Connecticut, eastern Pennsylvania, and Delaware. This vast area was called Lenapehoking or Land of the Lenape.

Mesingw (Me-sing): A Good Spirit Being who rode through the forest on the back of a huge deer, looking after the animals and protecting hunters and lost children.

Sakima (Sak-i-ma): A tribal leader or chief in peacetime

Shackamaxon (Shack-a-max-on): Located in the center of Lenapehoking where the Schuylkill River enters the Delaware, this large and prominent Lenape community was where tribal leaders met and important ceremonies took place for all Lenape.

Shamokin (Sha-mo-kin): Located where the two branches of the Susquehanna River converge, Shamokin was an important place of trade and cultural exchange for many Northeast Native American tribes, including the Lenape.

Wayhuhweehuhlahs (Way-huh-wee-huh-lah): The giver of names. A Lenape child was given a name around the age of five.